T0128864

# THE SILENT
## *Wolf*

DICK SCHOOF

ISBN: 978-1-4907-8248-5 (sc)
ISBN: 978-1-4907-8246-1 (e)

Library of Congress Control Number: 2017907517

*Trafford rev. 05/17/2017*

 www.trafford.com

**North America & international**
toll-free: 1 888 232 4444 (USA & Canada)
fax: 812 355 4082

I was cruising up the river searching for deer scent when I looked up rounding a bend in the narrow trail alongside the river and spotted the animal that walks upright, that I have called MAN. He was carrying a funny little stick in his hand and there he was right in front of me. Never have a been so scared to encounter a man so close to me. Fright, yes it was fright. What should I do? I stood in terror of this man that had invaded my home. What right did he have to come into my domain? I quickly melted in the brush alongside the trail and ran to the high ridge a short way downstream. There I sat and watched what the man would do. He stood there for some time and then finally started down the trail and went close to the water. Standing there, he began to throw a small object into the water and suddenly pulled out a nice fish. He did this a number of times as I watched him. Soon he had several fish that he put on a shiney string. These he carried back upstream to where he had a boat and it made a frightful roar. The boat then went up the lake and disappeared. Now I had my breath back and continued my search for deer to feed my pack. This is the job of the leader of the pack, feed the cubs and the adults. I'm called the Alpha Male. My pack calls me Argon.

As we sat by the fire after supper that night the wife said let's have a fish fry tomorrow evening. It sounded good to me so I readily agreed. Fresh fish right out of the water and in the pan is great eating. Days old fish that smells like fish, you can keep. Not my favorite food. I cooked fish the way I was taught by a great Canadian guide. Get your iron skillet good and hot with the lard almost smoking, then throw in the fillets of walleye that have been coated with egg and then breaded. Let them stay on one side counting to ten, flip them over and do the same. Be sure not to over do them. Are they ever great over an open fire alongside a beautiful Canadian lake. Yum yum, but back to my story. Next morning I arose early and headed down to the small lake called King Lake. the sun was just hitting the horizon as I silently left the campsite. Out on the lake I started the motor and puttered down through the twisting waterway. The sun glistened on the rising fog that swirled up from the warm water. Beautiful pink swirls and a loon whistling overhead. Down through the narrow rapids and on to the natural dam. There I pulled the boat up to shore and tied the painter to a tree. Grabbing my bag of lures and my rod I jumped out of the boat and started over the natural dam and down the trail alongside the river. The dew on the grass sparkled in the shafts of sunlight and wet my boots and pants as I started down the trail. The trail wound through the trees and bushes back aways from the small river. You could hear the roar of the water as it cascaded over the rocks that abounded in the water. Birds were singing their morning songs to add to the beauty of the wilderness. As I rounded a bend in the pathway through the woods I encountered a huge wolf. My first encounter with a wolf. Only knowing about Little Red Riding Hood, I WAS SCARED OUT OF MY WITS. What to do? Should I run? Should I pick up a stick to defend myself? No problem, he was gone, just seemed to dissolve into the brush. Soon the hair on the back of my neck went down and my heart stopped racing and I recovered y composure. So down the trail I went to my fishing spot at the second big pool in the river. This spot in Ontario, Canada is just loaded with smallmouth bass and in no time I had plenty of fish for supper. All the time I was casting for our meal I could feel the eyes of something watching me. I kept looking over my shoulder but could not discern anything.

Back I went to our camp on King Lake after threading my way through the rapids in the middle narrow part of the lake. Honey was happy that I had done the "honey do". Now we had the makings of a good supper of fresh bass that's my doing. Fillet the fish so there are no bones. Then egg and breadcrumbs set aside. Build up a big drift wood fire in the pit, get the lard in the big iron skillet and let it smoke. Yes, i said let it smoke so it's super hot. Then drop in the fillets, count to ten and turn them over for another ten and done. Put them aside as I add a large can of small potatoes and they are golden in a few minutes. Now eat hearty family!

Later that night as sweetheart and I sat around the fire I told her about my encounter with the huge wolf. Then we talked about excited our little dog got on several occasions when we motored close to the shore and truly had to restrain the animal from jumping out to go after some animal in the brush. Domestic dogs hate wolves and will try to go after them. Guess it was a wolf although we never saw one. It was a great day and it got me thinking. Wolves, and right where I go fishing. Maybe could study them. So, when I got back to civilization I started a concerted search of all the literature I could find. Most of the material I found was from Canada and Alaska, some of it very rewarding and intriguing. So I started my life ambition of studying wolves.

One of the most interesting things I found out about the much maligned wolf is that no wild, healthy wolf has ever attacked a human. There are no verified accounts of a wild, healthy wolf attacks on a human. So the stories of Little Red Riding Hood and The Three Pigs are just stories, and only that.

Literature wasn't enough for me so I decided to do some investigating for myself. At this point I was living in Upstate New York and only an hour drive from the Canadian border. That made it easy to get to the little trailer I had installed on a knowl close to King Lake. Yes, I had purchased a small trailer and insulated it to keep me arm in the middle of winter out in the BUSH of the Canadian wilds. I stocked it with plenty of dehydrated foods, a one hundred pound propane tank, a great heater, toilet seat to fit on a folding chair and I was ready to spend some time in the wilderness.

Never did I expect to have the air temperature drop to 64 degrees below zero.

So the first winter I got ready for my stay in the wilderness. I had cross country skis but had to buy snowshoes. Got me a pair of Pickeral style which are easier to get through brush. During the previous summer I had stocked the trailer with all the food I would need for a long stay. Since the trailer was some six miles from a plowed road, the toboggan I purchased would hold all of my immediate supplies as I cross country skied to my dwelling. Naturally I had a bottle of good brandy for snake bite protection. At the time I was selling cars in New York and my boss offered me an old used four wheel drive jeep with a top on back. He assured me that it would go through anything. Sure! So off I went one cold December day heading for the bush. Arriving at the dirt road to camp I found that I could drive the first few miles to the old log cabin of the owner. That much of the road had been plowed. Stopping at Law's cabin, we pass the time of day and then I announced that it was time to drive the next two miles to my camp. "Ain't been plowed" he said, "better not try it". But my boss had assured me that the jeep would go through anything. It started out great but soon bogged down in two feet of snow and a thick layer of ice under that. Took me half a day to dig out and turn around, fix two flats and drive the several hundred yards back to his cabin. Well I finally got to my abode using my sled and skis. Settled in with the heater turned on and soon had a comfortable and cosy room.

The trailer was twelve feet long and had a lower double bed, a two burner stove, an icebox and about six square feet of floor space. Some narrow but enough room to turn around in. There was a table that doubled as my desk and two bench chairs. I also had installed a small propane tank and a mantle burner for light over the table. Did that give off heat! That first night i went out to stand in the glistening snow under a bright moon and listened for my wolves. Didn't take long to hear them howling, so I answered them as best I could and to my great surprise they quickly answered me. I couldn't believe they were really talking to me so I started again and sure enough they howled back. After many nights of calling, as the years went by, the wolves actually would come by my camp to inspect me. Often they were no more than three feet away from me. Never a growl, never a threat in any way. In all the literature there has never been a verified attack on a human by a wild wolf. So again, Little Red Riding Hood is just a nice story, but not true.

Next morning after a hasty meal I went outside in the below zero temperature and donned my snowsuit and cross country skis. Down the winding road in deep snow, through the glistening snow covered hemlocks that covered the area to the dam that separated Crotch Lake from King Lake. At the ice covered lake I skied down the bank and out on the lake. Now as I got out on the snow covered lake I felt as though something was watching me. Turning to look back at the cabins on the hillside I could see nothing, just my imagination. Soon out on the broad expanse of the lake I found my first evidence of wolves. TRACKS! Yes, tracks, and they were big. No question they were wolves. So I followed them and they led to a stump sticking out of the frozen surface. The snow all around was yellow. They had peed all over it. Of course, this was a territory marker spot warning other wolf packs where their territory was. Don't come any closer. As I continued on I found scat, wolf poop, and put it in a sandwich bag to later inspect under the microscope to find out what the wolves were eating. The further I went I could see where they had marked their territory on a big rock. The play in the snow told a story of two cubs romping with their mother, the alpha female. In places I could see where they had stood up and tried to bite Momma on the neck. She was obviously very tolerant of their rough play. Now I started back toward the dam and up the snow covered dirt road to my camp. As I passed the rustic empty cabins I had that feeling that something was up in the woods watching me. I turned off the trail and climbed into the hemlocks. As I got some distance on the hillside there were the tracks of two wolves. Following them a short distance I found where they had both sat on their rear and watched me as I skied in their home. So back I went to my little camp and wrote down my observations.

Tina and her two cubs, Lucifer and Lona, were back at the denning area when Papa Argon returned with son Swift. They told of the man on the long sticks that followed Tina's track along with the two cubs. He didn't seem to pose any threat to us, and strangely picked up the poop, scat, of the youngsters and put it in a little clear bag. Very strange. Also he didn't carry one of those long sticks that made a terrible noise and flamed fire. Could he be a safe one as the summer people seem to be? He called to us the previous night and we replied with no bad effects so I guess he's alright. Next time he calls to us I will go to his camp and carefully go close to him making sure he doesn't have one of those sticks that spit fire in his hand. So the next night at dusk when he gave our call I went close to his camp and gingerly padded close to him and he sat still. Never moved at all and made no move to attack me. What a relief not to have those groups of men that shoot the deer and us anytime they get the chance. They killed Uncle Luna two years ago with their fire sticks. We tried to rouse him but the red blood kept seeping out of him and he soon started to get cold. We had to leave him in the woods.

Winter is our best time of year with the deep snow on the ground. Argon goes out and finds a deer that is crippled or very old that we can catch easily. Poppa calls us and directs us to a post where we will wait. Then he goes back to the target animal and drives it to us. When the deer comes by us we all chase it until it falls to the ground or we pull it down and kill it. Then we stand back while Argon and Tina have their fill. Then it's our turn after the rest of the adults eat. We soon learn that the soft insides are the easiest to eat and we push our heads into the body cavity to eat the soft tissue. Our ruff is covered with blood and gore and soon gets to stinking. That's why our relatives, the dog, love to roll in bad smelling things. When we got our fill of the venison we would go off a short distance and dig a hole in the ground and turn our bellies out and put all the food we had eaten in the hole. Then we'd cover it up and go back for more. Finally, it was time to curl up and sleep. Then back to the carcass and do the same thing again. The rest of the carcass was hidden under some brush to save for the next meal. Eat when you can or else go hungry.

We have a number of other rules that we learned as cubs. Momma and Poppa eat first at any kill. I guess that's because Momma will need the strength for the cubs developing in her belly and Poppa must be ready to find more food for our pack. It also is a rule that only Momma and Poppa mate. When the cubs are born in the Spring while she is carefully left at the entrance of the den. Another is that when our alpha male calls us we must obey instantly. When Momma, our alpha female, comes out of the den with the new cubs. After introductions, Tina goes off on a toot in the territory, kills a deer and gorges. In the meantime, we all must take care of the new ones. They love to wander so they must be brought back to the den. They must be fed and kept clean. Oh, to endure their constant biting of our legs and neck. They seem to be all over us, they are the new members of our family.

Winter was soon upon us in upstate New York so I started preparing for my fifth trip into the bush of Ontario. My trailer had been stocked with all the dehydrated food stuffs I could think of. Time to travel on. So one bright morning I drove North to the Thousand Island Bridge over the Sharbot Lake. Now on into the bush to my little camp. By now I had the routine down pretty well so I felt less like a rookie as I did a number of years ago. Stopped at the log cabin of the owner and had him bring me up on all the events of the past few months. Now on to my shanty and fire up the propane heater to get the icicles off the surroundings. Not a soul for twenty miles except my friend in the cabin. Talk of quiet and solitude. You could hear a pine needle drop. Skiing from that cabin I had frozen some, so of course I had to have a short snort of the snake bite medicine. That warmed my gut. Now it was close to midnight so out onto the snow covered slope and I called to "MY" wolves. Sure enough they responded almost at once. The entire pack got in the mood and all started singing back to me. Gosh that's a pretty sound coming through the hemlocks, with the moonlight shining on the pristine snow. As I stood there in the cold of a winter night, an owl flew by with it's wings whirring softly. Surely it was searching for a mouse to pop its head out of the snow. Soon I heard the pack calling back and forth as they obeyed Argons call to follow a weak deer. Across the lower King Lake ice they howled and on up to the bug lake, Crotch Lake. Suddenly the calls changed and I could discern that they had made a kill. The calling had stopped and surely they were eating their fill of a venison supper. Now it was time to hit the sack. I could check on the kill tomorrow morning. I checked the temperature as I got to my abode. The mercury sat at 12 degrees below zero. That dry cold of the North is so much different than the cold, moist air of the lower forty eight. Up with the sun I polished off two packages of oatmeal softened with boiling water. That should stick to the ribs for a day in the bush. Put on my skis and started down the snow covered dirt road. Hemlocks hung heavy with snow across the road and make a beautiful picture. The mice had been out and made their trails under the rail fence bordering the road. Then I spotted a rabbit track just behind the fence. There it stopped and the wing imprints of a red tailed hawk had swooped down and got his meal. Had to be a red tailed hawk because they were the only ones I saw around the area. Got to the dam separating the two lakes and stood for a moment to enjoy the huge expanse of the pristine wilderness. Not a soul, not a sound of humans, just wilderness and beauty! Skiing up the big lake I tried to find the kill from the last nights chase by the pack. Searching back and forth I finally found the bloody snow and there was the carcass, pretty well eaten. After taking my pictures I backed off as quickly as I could so as not to bother my pack. Now back to the warmth of my camp and a bite to eat. Yes, more dehydrated food. I sat down at my little table and wrote my notes of last night and today. Tonight it's getting much colder and the wolves didn't respond to my call. So off to bed I went to get some extra hours of sleep. Got up to bone chilling cold and then I checked the temperature and it was a frosty 64 degrees below zero.

Today I had planned to go to the upper lake and follow a small stream that wound into the lake. As I expected, it quickly opened up to a wide swampy area with many tree stumps all over. The dead trees had many huge nests in their tops. They were the nests of the great blue heron. Searching for several miles I found no evidence of my pack. So I returned to the main lake and searched further on. Crossing the large expanse of the lake, I came to the area called The Three Sisters, where a piece of land juts out into the lake and here I found many tracks of wolves and a number of deer. I followed a set of tracks where two wolves had followed a deer. It was obvious that the deer had started to run with the wolves right after it. The deer was making long strides and as it bounded over a fallen log it had slipped and fallen on its side. It must have rebounded quickly and run on leaving the wolves behind, for they soon gave up the chase. The snow told the tale. By now the cold had gotten to me and I started for my little camp on the hill for some warmth. As I traveled back to camp along the snow covered dirt road there were the tracks of the field mice as they came up out of the deep snow to scurry under the crisscrossed split rail fence in search of what ever. Back in camp it was time to write in my ledger of the day's happenings. That night the moon shone and the stars twinkled and each step in the snow crunched in the extreme cold. The snow glistened in the moonlight. I called to the wolf pack and in a few minutes I heard a chorus responding to me. What a beautiful sound. Now off to sleep.

Dehydrated foods are great to keep you going. In fact, one trail mix spaghetti dinner is as good as any homemade sauce I have ever tasted. However, a solid piece of meat is mighty welcome after eating dehydrated food for a time. So this winter I decided to bring some ice fishing gear along. Packed my plastic sled with my gear and started for the lower lake. Couldn't get on the ice near the spillway since the strong current kept it ice free close to the dam. I walked the shore line for some distance and then got on the ice and proceeded about halfway down the lake. Found a spot near the small island that I knew had produced fish in the summer, so I started to set up for fishing there. Got the ice auger out if the sled and started to cut a hole in the ice. To my great surprise the auger broke through after only a few turns. Gosh!! Only half an inch of ice. Get gone from here before you fall though! So I quickly backtracked in my snowy tracks and got off the lake. That was a close one. I never realized that the current from the dam would flow down the lake that far and keep the ice from freezing in that extreme cold. Lucky I didn't fall through because there was no one to help me for several miles. That was my last try at fresh meat.

It was in early winter that Gigi and Swift were searching for deer near the log cabin of the man who stayed there all year. As they walked to an open field a boom sounded and Gigi jumped in the air and landed on her side. Red fluid gushed out of a hole in her side. I raced over to her side and tried to get her up but she couldn't move. I pleaded with her to get up but she didn't seem to hear me. Then I heard another boom and the snow by my feet exploded in a shower so I ran away as fast as I could. Back I went to our pack and told of Gigi's loss. Argon reminded us to stay away from where the man with the long stick that made a loud noise and spit flame lived. Poof, Gigi was no longer with us.

Spring came and I made my early trip to Crotch Lake for my fishing for the succinct walleyes. Early in the morning I took the boat out and motored through the early morning mist that swirled in beautiful pink swirls to the area we called The Three Sisters. There I started to jig for the great eating walleye pike. Cast the jog with a nightwalker attached as far as you can and let it sink to the bottom. Then start to retrieve the lure in a slow up and down motion, when you feel a slight resistance wait for a count of three and then strike hard. Now comes the fight, for the walleye is a strong fighter. Across a short bay from the Three Sisters is a long narrow split of land stretching out in the lake. Tina had taken her three cubs out on this land at the same time I was fishing.

Well the cubs started trying to howl the way the adults did. They squeaked, they stuttered, shrieked and I have never heard anything so funny in my life. I rolled on the bottom of the boat until my sides hurt. Those little darlings made my day. Until this day I can still laugh at the memory of the sounds they made trying to imitate their parents.

Back the following winter I was ready to start a new time with my wolves. So up through the Thousand Islands and on to Crotch Lake, nice name! The snow was deep and as usual the temperature was near zero. Got the heater going and put away the few supplies I could carry on the plastic kids orange toboggan. Started for the lake to check things out but as soon as I rounded a small bend on top of a small rise I spotted a number of tracks in the snow. So I got off my skis and started to check them out. A red squirrel was followed by a fisher, and they were followed by a wolf. Well the red squirrel jumped into a pine tree, raced up the trunk and jumped to another tree. Then it jumped to the snow and raced for another tree followed by the fisher. The trail told the story of the fisher following the red squirrel and both being chased by the wolf. It appeared that the squirrel got away but the fisher made lunch for the wolf. That night I sat in a chair outside in the snow and cold as the stars twinkled and the snow glistened in the moonlight and called for my pack. Moments later I heard the answering calls. So I sat waiting. Soon I spotted movement in the woods and the entire pack came by me, no more than five feet away. There has never been any threat to me by the wolves. I carry no weapons or anything to protect myself. The wolves just seemed to say hello as they passed by and moved off to their own doings. I feel perfectly safe in the bush many miles from any habitation.

Time for some fun in the deep snow. Took the plastic sled to a nearby hill and with my big boots on I tromped up the snow up the hill. Then up and down several times to make a trough in the snow. At the top of the hill I sat in the sled and slowly slid to the bottom of the hill. After doing this several times I had a pretty good sled run. My partner got in the sled and started down the hill with the dog barking after her. She raced to the bottom at a pretty good clip. After several runs by both of us we had a fair luge and we whipped down the hill at a good clip. I measured the distance from the top of the hill to the bottom and then timed my partner's speed down the hill. We got up to 67 miles per hour racing down the hill. Breathtaking in that little sled. Plenty of time for play and we were tired that night and slept like babies.

Bathing was a bit of a problem. Can't go out to the stream and go for a dip, so we set up a tub big enough to stand in. Heated a pot of water on the stove and poured it over the body. Not the greatest bath but we got some cleaner. Enough so that we could stand the smell. Food in the camp turned out to be quite good. The dehydrated foods were very tasty and plenty of nourishment. On a rare occasion we skied out to the car and drove to town about forty miles away and bought some fresh meats and veggies to please our palate. The town of Perth had several nice restaurants so we enjoyed a sit down meal. Then back to camp for some more time with our pack. The country road offered some interesting sights. Up ahead as we rounded a bend sat a beautiful redtail hawk, so we slowed to a stop to watch him from a distance. His head turned as he scanned the ground below. Down he flew, or dived, and pounced on some unsuspecting rodent that had popped up out of the deep snow blanket. Supper in his talons he rose majestically to the wire he had started from. On down the six miles of dirt road that was covered with snow to the end of the plowed stretch. Then we loaded the plastic sled with our supplies and skied back to the snug camp on the hill.

Spring was approaching and the pack had wintered over on venison. Lucifer was concerned about momma Tina. He went to sister Lona and asked what was wrong with Tina? Momma wasn't allowing them to play and nip at her ruff any more. Lona thought it had something to do with her belly becoming distended. Then too she seemed to spend a lot of time dragging grass and bits of fur into the underground den. Then she disappeared in the den and didn't come out at all. Now all the adults started bringing food to the den entrance and pushing it inside. They were feeding Momma. Finally the snow was gone and we could hear the squeaking of little voices from the den. A bit later Momma brought out three little cubs, our new brother and sisters. Their eyes were barely open and Momma carried each one in her mouth and put them in front of Poppa. We all got an introduction to the new members of our family. Gorgie and Gigi now took over the new kids as Momma disappeared. Off she went and some time later we heard her make a kill. She must have found an old and feeble deer to bring down herself. Enjoying her release from the den she howled in pleasure and gorged out on fresh venison. She was gone for two days while the rest of the pack enjoyed taking care of the three cubs. Roll, nip, and play. Other than eating, that's all they wanted to do. In no time they were racing around the den area and straying. So each one of us had to go and bring them back home. What little pests.

It was so time consuming to cross country ski to the far end of the great lake to follow the tracks of "my" wolves that I decided to try to find a SkiDoo to use for quick trips down the lake. Money was my big problem with only a teachers pension so I had to find something reasonable. Luck would have it that a friend knew a friend that had one of the first made SkiDoos and only wanted a small sum to get rid of it. Now I had wheels, skis with a motor. That fall I borrowed a pickup truck and took my SkiDoo to my camp in the "BUSH", and left it for my return in the winter. Never paid much attention to the loose gas cap. Snows came and unbeknownst to me siphoned into the gas tank. Winter arrived and I was back in camp. Tried to start the motor but no luck. Finally got Delmar, the caretaker and mechanic to have a look. The first thing he did was look at the gas cap. Pulled it off and turned the machine over and dumped all the watered gas out. Now the motor started after a few pulls on the starter rope. Yes of course, a fresh tank of gas. The carburetor on this old machine was held on with two screws that were impossible to get at, so if they loosened you had to reach inside the tricky thing and tighten them with your fingernail. Fun! I found this out the hard way when I was way down the lake, miles from my camp. The motor sputtered and coughed then caught for a while and then quit dead. After much investigating I found the problem and hand tightened the screws. What a relief, I thought I was stuck miles from the camp. I was soon swishing across the snow covered lake to investigate more tracks of my wolf pack and collect anything they left behind. Now I spotted a fresh track of a large deer that was being chased by one wolf. The deer was making huge leaps and so was a healthy animal. That wolf was out of luck. No healthy deer can ever be caught by a wolf, but as the deer ran and jumped over a fallen log it slipped and went down in a heap in the snow. I could see where it had gotten up, shook off the snow, and bounded on leaving the wolf in the dust. Oops, snow. Yes, the wolf only catches the old, the sickly, or the young. This helps to control the size of the deer herd and improve the genetic makeup of those animals. So back to camp to write in my journal of the day's events. A slug of snake bite medicine warmed me up as I broke out the dehydrated spaghetti and baked a biscuit. Now it was time to sit outside to enjoy the wilderness. Later I went outside to enjoy the full moon and the light glistening on the new snow. Soon the pack started to sing their lovely songs and I responded. The pack was so used to my being in their territory that they soon came calling. The entire pack came by only a few feet from where I stood on top of my knowl. They were saying howdy to a friend. They seemed to know I was not one of the hunters that shot them. Great evening, and now off to bed as the temperature dropped to twenty one below zero. The dry cold of this area is easy to take but you must keep all body parts covered. A face mask is a must. The cloth that touches your skin must have the property to wick away your sweat. This will keep you warm in the coldest weather.

Uncle Aluma told Argon that he had spotted a deer that was dragging a leg and making very slow progress through the snow. Argon quickly organized our hunt. Each one of us had a certain job to do. Some of us were posted at strategic spots along the path that Poppa would chase the deer. As the deer approached each one of us, we would take up the chase until the deer was exhausted. Then we pulled it down and quickly put it out of its misery. Now Argon and Tina started to eat as we all watched and waited for our turn. We all filled our bellies, went off a short distance, dug a small pit and emptied our bellies in the pit. That food was then covered over and back we went for a new belly full. After several such regurgitating stops we ate our fill and curled up for a nice nap on a full belly. Before Argon and Tina took their nap they carried the remains of the deer off to a little depression and put the deer in it and then covered it with brush. Now we had several places to fill our bellies when hunger struck us.

The river starts just below the natural dam at the end of King Lake. It probably averages about 25 feet across. In some places it widens greatly and makes large ponds. In many places it is a boulder strewn, rushing, white water stream. It's impossible to cross the river so you stay on one side. The water is clear and slightly brownish. All along the bank you can find smallmouth bass and walleye pike. Living in the rushing water they are the strongest of fighters.

There are no real paths as you start down river, so you have to pick your way through the brush and forest. About a half mile down the river there is a widening of the stream and a long narrow rock ledge alongside the water. This ridge supports the biggest population of Bottled Gentian I have ever seen. There amongst the Gentian are the Cardinal Flowers. The red and blue are the most attractive. The Gentians are rare but farther down river on the opposite shore there is a half acre of Ebony ferns that stand over a foot tall. A mile below the dam is the only place to cross the river when the river is low. Below that spot is a widening of the river into a real lake. Otter Lake here you may find a few pike. All this area is covered with pine, poplar and hardwood trees. This forest supports many kind of animal life.

One morning my son and I went down the river to catch some fish for an evening fish fry.

We had taken a bagged lunch so we could stay awhile. Had a grand time catching a mess of smallmouth bass and a couple of walleyes. But as you are having a ball the time slippes by. So now it was time to put on the food bag. We found a cozy spot where we could rest our backs against a big rock and see the water. As we munched on our sandwiches and slurped our soda, we chatted about our favorite Crotch Lake area. A movement along the shore and a porky came waddling towards us with not a care in the world. Our legs were outstretched and low and behold he, or she, waddled right over our legs. It never even realized we were there, so much for dangerous animals. Shortly after lunch we had caught a mess of fish and headed up river to our camp. As we approached the big pool just below the natural dam we heard a wolf calling and other wolves responding. The wolf calls were getting louder so we hid in some brush and waited. A deer went bounding upstream on the other side from our location. In the riverside brush we observed the deer racing through the brush, tongue hanging out of her mouth. Seconds later a lone wolf followed. That wolf was silent but we could hear the wolves on the points hollering to keep it running. Now an occasional bark from the animals at various spots along the expected trail and the deer was pushed on. In the quiet of the wilderness we could suddenly hear the howl of the kill, the wolves had their supper and then some. Wolves have to make a living, but it's not an eight to five job. So my son and I continued on with our catch back to camp. The wife was thrilled with the catch but more thrilled with our account of the wolves.

The winter was upon me in upstate and I headed for Canada and my wolves. This was to be a very cold winter. After passing the time of day with the owner I skied to my camp. Sat down to a hasty meal and I put away the food. Next morning I was up early and soon out on the lake. Scanning the distant shore line I spotted several deer feeding in the brush. Now, I thought, this is my chance to watch the wolf pack in their attempt to make a kill. What strategy would they use? So i climbed a rocky outcrop of rose quartz along a nearby shore. I had my pack with two sandwiches and a thermos of hot beef bullion so I could stay for quite some time, never mind the temperature, which hovered at 12 degrees below zero. I was in my snug insulated suit. I found a cozy spot in the rocks and settled in to watch for developments. So for the next four hours I watched the deer as they browsed on the tips of saplings. But no wolves. The cold penetrated to my bones and I finally gave up my spot in the rocks and climbed down to the snow covered ice. Crossing the inlet I was on

I climbed the far bank and entered the thick brush only to find a wolf had sat on his rear watching me in my hidden rock den. So smart? So back I skied to my cozy camp to lick my wounded pride.

Yes the wolf is a brilliant animal. They have a very close knit family order. The alpha male, Argon and the alpha female Tina are the only ones that mate. This is a means of controlling the size of the pack. In times of famine the alpha female will only have two cubs and if the food source is very low she may reabsorb all the embryos in her body. When she is in the last stages of pregnancy she will stay in her den and all the adults will bring her food. Then finally after birth a few weeks later she will bring out the cubs for inspection. After all the relations have made their inspection she bounds off and goes on a tour of the territory, kills some animal and has a feast. She just needs to get away from the little darlings. She might be gone from the pack for two to three days. Interesting how the relations, alpha male Argon, grandpa Max, sister and brother Gigi and Swift, yes even the cubs help take care of the newborns.

To this day the much maligned wolf has never had a verified account of attacking a person. So Little Red Riding Hood and The Three Little Pigs are cute stories but have no evidence to support the wolves actions.

One summer day I was on my usual fishing trip to the "bush country". In late afternoon I parked my boat on a secluded beach and climbed a nearby hillside and stretched out in the sun. No sounds other than the birds singing. Almost asleep I noticed some movement in a nearby grassy area. Then I spotted one of my wolves on his belly inching his way through the grass. This was in late summer and grasshoppers were in their last instar. They had shed their last exoskeleton and could now fly. The wolf made a quick jump forward with both paws together and landed on a hopper. I watched for half an hour while he caught and consumed twenty or more hoppers.

So the wolf is a very adaptable animal and will make use of any foodstuffs. When I returned to my laboratory from wintertime with the scat examined under the microscope I find nothing but deer hair and deer bone bits.

The wolf is a beautiful animal and forms a true family group. They work together and in their own way aid in the balance of nature making a stronger deer population.

Printed in the United States
By Bookmasters